Ants

Rebecca Rissman

www.raintreepublishers.co.uk
Visit our website to find out more information about Raintree books.

To order:
☎ Phone 0845 6044371
🖨 Fax +44 (0) 1865 312263
💻 Email myorders@raintreepublishers.co.uk

Customers from outside the UK please telephone +44 1865 312262

Raintree is an imprint of Capstone Global Library Limited, a company incorporated in England and Wales having its registered office at 7 Pilgrim Street, London, EC4V 6LB – Registered company number: 6695582

Text © Capstone Global Library Limited 2013
First published in hardback in 2013
The moral rights of the proprietor have been asserted.

Edited by Dan Nunn, Rebecca Rissman, and Catherine Veitch
Designed by Joanna Hinton-Malivoire
Picture research by Mica Brancic
Originated by Capstone Global Library Ltd
Production by Victoria Fitzgerald
Printed in China by South China Printing Company Ltd

ISBN 978 1 406 24130 3
16 15 14 13 12
10 9 8 7 6 5 4 3 2 1

British Library Cataloguing in Publication Data
Rissman, Rebecca.
Ants. – (Creepy crawlies)
595.7'96-dc22
A full catalogue record for this book is available from the British Library.

Acknowledgements
We would like to thank the following for permission to reproduce photographs: Dreamstime p. 23 (© Alexey Fedorov); FLPA p. 11a (Minden Pictures/Piotr Naskrecki); iStock p. 21 (© arlindo71); Shutterstock pp. 3 & 11 left (© Doug Lemke), 5, 22 (© Jens Stolt), 7 (© Evgeniy Ayupov), 8 (© Marek Lambert), 9 (© Kesu); 10a (© Andrey Pavlov), 10b (© Kurt G), 11b (© Hue Chee Kong), 13 (© Asharkyu), 15 (© Jetsetmodels), 16 (© Eric Isselée), 17 (© Juha Sompinmäki), 19 (© D. Kucharski & K. Kucharska), 20 (© Shalex84), 22 (© Peter Waters), 22 (© Photolinc), 22 & 5 (© Jens Stolt), 23 (© Alex Staroseltsev), 23 (© Irin-k).

Cover photograph of an ant reproduced with permission of Shutterstock (© Pixelman).

Every effort has been made to contact copyright holders of any material reproduced in this book. Any omissions will be rectified in subsequent printings if notice is given to the publisher.

The publishers would like to thank Michael Bright for his assistance in the preparation of this book.

Contents

Let's search!

Let's search for creepy crawlies.
Look under plants here and there.

What creatures did you find?
Little ants are everywhere!

Look a bit closer.
How many parts do you see?

An ant has more than one body part!
Count them: 1, 2, 3!

7

It's got six little legs.
Can you count each one?

1, 2, 3, 4, 5, and 6!
Counting legs is fun!

Most ants are brown or black.
But some are red or green!

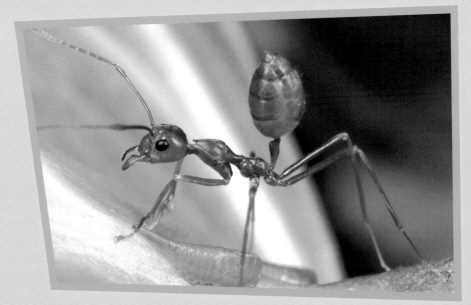

What's the brightest coloured ant that you have ever seen?

Stomp! Stomp! Stomp!
Ants like to march in line.

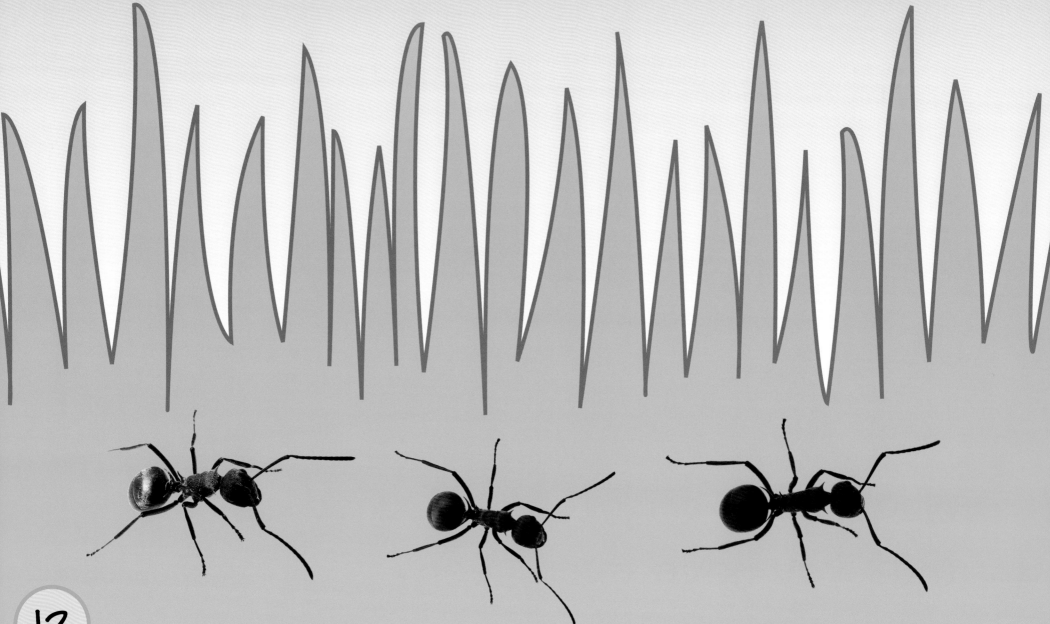

They march through the grass
in super-speedy time!

When ants feel hungry, what do they like to eat?

Fruit, leaves, and other bugs, or anything that's sweet!

honey

15

Have you ever seen an ant carrying a leaf in its jaws?

When a queen ant has babies,
she has quite a few!

They hatch from eggs as larvae
and ants give them food to chew.

larvae

Some ants live in anthills.
Other ants live in nests.

Some don't even have a home.
They think moving around is best!

Counting ants

How many ants are on these two pages? Try to count each one.

Look around the rocks and flowers.
Counting ants is fun!

Answer: five ants.

Did you know?

If food is too big for an ant to carry back to the nest, the ant finds another ant to help it carry the food.

Index